Now, looking back, going forward –
a journey of wellbeing through schizophrenia

Anne-Louise Lowrey

Published by Anne-Louise Lowrey
Publishing partner: Paragon Publishing, Rothersthorpe

First published 2021

ISBN 978-1-78222-822-6

Book design, layout and production management by Into Print
www.intoprint.net
+44 (0)1604 832149

CONTENTS

INTRODUCTION

When asked by my daughter, Anne-Louise to write an introduction to her book – *Now, looking back, going forward* – I was unsure as to whether or not, it was a wise thing for me to do. Being her mother, I felt in a sense, too close to the situation. On the other hand – for the same reasons – who better?

Looking again at the title, *Now, looking back, going forward*, it seems very appropriate, because it really has been a long journey, going back more than 30 years. Indeed, so awful were some of the happenings back then – one simply wanted to forget them, bury them, wipe them out.

But now I'm glad to say, I can recall them with some gratitude, because Anne-Louise, who suffered greatly over the years, is a wonderful person, loved by all who know her. I won't go into details of what she went through. She will tell you that herself in the book.

Suffice to say, that of all the trials and tribulations her dad and I went through at the time, nothing was worse than seeing your child, whom you love unreservedly, going through hell, and feeling there was nothing you could do to help.

Let's just say, once she had started the long journey back, it really was like the proverbial – 'climbing up from the dark valley to the sunny uplands.'

Now, looking back, going forward

THIS IS ABOUT my well-being journey, where I am now, where I have come from and where I want to be in the future. I believe that everyone has the right to enjoy and improve their health, regardless of the obvious differences in any society, like income, culture, education and disability.

For many years I thought that I was unable to stop smoking because I have schizophrenia and during the eighties and nineties, when I was an in-patient in hospital, smoking was endemic among the mental health community. When first being treated with depixol injection, my smoking doubled within the space of a few weeks and my weight increased. I was tired and lethargic all the time, unable to walk the long distances that had kept me fit prior to being admitted. However, it wasn't all bad, and I started to work in the hospital garden– it was called *Sprout Market Garden*. I was often the soup maker there, and all my adult life I have taken great pleasure in making soup, even though housekeeping and organisation have always been a struggle for me.

My fantastic dad taught me to make soup when I was a child, with the vegetables he grew in the garden or allotment. We had always joined in with soup making when we were little, either grating carrots or peeling potatoes. He was a nurseryman to trade and I spent a lot of time with him in the garden and kitchen. He made soup all year round, no matter what the weather, until he died in 2018. I intend to keep his tradition going.

We're currently in lockdown April 2020, and never has health been so much on the mind of everyone. Not only the Covid19 virus, but actually how to keep physically and mentally fit while spending so much time indoors and away from much needed and appreciated family and friends. I've never been much of a television person, but I have used YouTube for years – mostly yoga classes and music, as well as motivational talks. At the moment, my computer is even more important and has become my lifeline, just helping me to stay connected.

However, a more important lifeline to me over the years has been the NHS. I am more than happy to applaud them and all workers every Thursday evening. I was born at home, delivered by a midwife and had an illness-free childhood, thanks to vaccinations and excellent general practice care throughout. In my teens and early twenties, mental illness crept in and I spent time in the Royal Edinburgh Hospital. It wasn't easy and I resented the doctors in particular, because they wielded so much power. I felt friendless and on the outside of society, 'left out' and angry a lot of the time. But these feelings eventually passed as the people I met through this episode in my life were to become great friends and acquaintances within a supportive and vibrant community.

My stopping smoking also bears the mark of extremely patient and dedicated NHS smoking cessation workers, considering that it took around ten attempts for me to finally succeed and they never once wrote me off. They always maintained it was possible. As well as this, every fortnight for more than thirty years, I have visited the practice nurse for my injection of depixol and it's a crucial part of my routine. So, I have everything to thank the NHS for and it is a fact that I would have come to a lot of harm without them, and probably wouldn't be here.

So, I'm starting with poetry that was either written recently or reflects how I've been feeling recently. This is the 'now' part of the book of wellbeing and trying to stay healthy in unprecedented times. I'm feeling dusty and making daily calls to either breathing space, Edinburgh crisis centre or Samaritans to cope with the lack of contact and feelings of being cooped up. I'm not completely alone but isolating with my partner. We don't usually live together but have teamed up to get through this strange situation which feels unreal.

Now

Now

Is now
Our time?
Not a future memory
Of parties
Or paddling in the sea
The fear of losing loved ones
Is it selfish
Just to be?

Is now
The moment
We were all born for?
Our climate
Our blame
The world kindles energy
Feeds the flame

Our fire, our hope
I hear the rain
Faintly
Cold puddles are forming
On the pavement
Beside the kerb
And in potholes

I hear the rain
And the inner repetition
Of my own prayers

Imagine having
No one to love
Or resent?
No garlicky kisses
Not guilty
Nothing to repent

And now
That cholesterol and sugar
Are no longer the enemies
We'll have ice-cream
Every day!

Something else
Will take us away

Is now the time
We could and should?
Come together
For the common good

Sitting here

I'm sitting here
Feeling fine
Bag of crisps
Glass of wine

And yet I know
I can't go out
There's something big
To worry about

It somehow feels
Quite surreal
I hear the seagulls
Shriek and squeal

I'm dying to go
To work today
See my friends
Kirkgate café
Full of toddlers
Hard at play

And take off
To the countryside
As if there was
No need to hide

I'm suffering
From laziness
Sick, fed up
This haziness

A microscopic
Plague, disease
Leaves us all
Ill at ease

With any kind
Of touch or hug
We'll surely catch
The deadly bug

Wash our hands
It's really crucial
Not one of us
Is somehow special

Charlie, warley
Boris, Matt
Not living in
A council flat

They've caught the lurgy
Nonetheless
With life conditions
Of the best

I'm down today
Must pick me up
Must see it as
A HALF FULL cup

I've got my home
The internet
My yoga and
I'm not in debt
(touch wood!!!)

So really
I am overflowing
Perhaps this time
Can be spent growing

So here's to us!
The human race
We've made mistakes
It's our disgrace

But we're good people
In the main
I must believe
We'll try again

Thinking of
Our friend the earth
Let's make this time
To show our worth

What to do?

Nothing to write about
No work to do
No interactions
Nothing new

No soup to make
No rhubarb to stew
No weeds to pull
No coffee to brew

No scones to bake
No soil to rake
No heather bed
No garden tool shed

No football, no racing
No parties or barbeques
No weddings or funerals
Just relentless bad news

But, there are hoverflies
A cracking top floor view
Blossom and blue skies

Dandelions, digitalis
Deer and foxes too
Strolling around
In an open zoo

I'll telephone my mother
My neighbours, my friends
Every day till the lockdown ends

I'll skype, I'll type
Get into the hype
Stay safe, paint a rainbow
Applaud from the window

Will it be weeks
Months
Or a year?

Going mad is a genuine fear

Something Nice

Think of something nice
Like a butterfly
A cushie doo
A spicy apple pie

A piece of cake
A pasta bake
A sunny, cloudless sky

A morning walk
My uncle Jock
With his bees
And heather honey

Arthur's seat
Dunsape loch
A cuddly, bouncing bunny

And now the spring
Is underway
The fresh, green buds
Cheer up the day

Looking forward
To the brightness
The longer days
The newness, lightness

Summer's coming
Bees are humming
Jack Frost is fast asleep
The grass is grown
The seeds are sown
Pile up the compost heap

So here's to now
It's time to bow
To nature's paradise

Accept our lot
Love what we've got
It surely will suffice

So …
I'll clear my head
Jump out of bed
And think of something nice

Making Soup

The joy of making soup's well known
Of chopping veg your dad has grown
Selecting little cuts of meat
Or a healthy vegetarian treat

Bacon, lentil, chilli, kale
Tattie and pepper, hearty and hale

Singing songs by Leonard Cohen
Woodie Guthrie and Bob Dylan
You sing while your creation bubbles
Simmering down all your troubles

And when your kitchen fills with steam
You drink a cup of tea and dream
Of all the different combinations
Ingredients from many nations

That you can mingle altogether
To be enjoyed in any weather

In hope of peace

I'm a coward I suppose
Weak
I enjoy life
Maybe you'd laugh at me
For being mild and meek

I want it to stop
End the killing
Instead let's grow crops

I don't want to use nerve gas
Chemical weapons
Air strikes
Interrogation sessions

Tit for tat

Terrorism
State aggression
Racist nationalism

Divide and rule
Blame each other
Trust the fool
Betray your brother

I enjoy reading
And drinking wine
Coffee, tea and water, sometimes

Weeding seedlings
And patio paving
Satisfying desires
And human cravings

Chopping vegetables
Eating fruit
Trying to be sensible
Cleaning my walking boots

God forbid
If we were all at war
Nothing but fear
To get up in the morning for

Can't we gather together
And stop the tide
Of mindless hatred
And thought divide

Let's say no to killing
All of us
Don't believe that war is thrilling
It's cruel and unjust

I'm sitting at home
Warm and dry
Comfortably alone
And ill-prepared to die

Death of a hoverfly

I hurt a hoverfly
Broke its wing
While I was weeding
So I put it
On a buttercup to die

I thought at least
It might just have a chance
Somewhere beautiful
To make its final stance

Sweet nectar to drink
A quiet place
To rest and think

About the future
Of the earth
A pollinator
Has its worth

Yet if I can grieve
So small a life
What about deforestation, abbatoirs
And human strife?

Is earthly death
Just an interruption?
Black lives matter
End the corruption!

Does life go on and on
Into the afterworld
Reborn

If I can be so kind today
Heeding what the vegans say
And worry what the rhinos think
While animals become extinct

I want to save orangutans
There's no doubt about that
But can I help the human?
The unimportant as a gnat

Some lives are seen
As trivial, expendable
Like a single, injured hoverfly
Not worth preserving
What does that say of us?
Which of us is deserving?

Harvest Sunday

This is my journal
All about me
My hopes and dreams
I'm important you see

I wonder what
The world will say
On waking to
This brand new day

The sun is risen
Yet I feel lost
The morning's christened
With a little frost

I'll see you Jesus
At eleven
Seated happily
In heaven

The harvest gathered
Autumn gold
Still I'm bothered
By pains of old

Like us all
I love earth's beauty
I hear the call
To do my duty

Do I listen?
I wish I could
I'm often driven
By my mood

Lockdown blues
Can't watch the news
Everyone has
Different views

I want to find
Some common ground
Some like of mind
Some safe and sound

I hope when this
Pandemic ends
We'll love each other
Make amends

Debating about
Who is right
Can separate us
Cause a fight

Perhaps we never
Will agree
The human race
Our thoughts are free

So morning,
Evening
Every day
I'll bow my little head
And pray

ANOTHER VITAL INGREDIENT in my life I'm afraid to say, has been the welfare state. Much berated are we long-term sick people by the workers who pay the taxes, and I really want to say 'thank you' it is appreciated. Sometimes people are quite angry and vicious about it and I often feel suicidal when this happens. I try to contribute by volunteering in my local community café and local community allotment. I strive to be a good citizen and hopefully I am not a drain on society, as I sometimes feel when I look at the news or facebook posts from people with strong right-wing beliefs.

However, I am not about to peddle politics, but it does upset and worry me and I struggle to keep up with working and tax paying. I am not a Communist and I don't believe everything should be controlled by the state. I think we need a mixture of public services and private businesses to have a healthy society. People need to be creative and to strive for goals, but we still need a health service, education, libraries, parks, museums and transport to be available free at the point of use or at an affordable cost to ordinary people.

I have always volunteered all my life but rarely had paid work, as it was often too difficult and demanding for me and I became ill – so volunteering seemed a good way of putting something back into society, and of course, I get a lot out of it too. Here is a poem about the wonderful Kirkgate café at Liberton in Edinburgh.

Ode to Kirkgate Café

We're all a bunch
Of volunteers
Serving lunch
This past few years

At Liberton Kirkgate
Café community
Where we work hard
And celebrate unity

When life is good
We cruise along
But equally
When things go wrong
The Kirkgate spirit
Keeps us strong

Our manager
Norma Brown
Will pick you up
When you are down

Along with chefs
Baristas, bakers
Waiting staff
And toastie makers
Washing dishes
Can be fun
At Kirkgate café
Work gets done

We've got our customers to praise
When they come in on quiet days
As well as times
When we are stretched
They're patient then
And don't get vexed

The little toddlers
Squeal and play
They brighten up
Most any day

For those of us
A little older
As winter draws
And winds grow colder

It gives us somewhere
Warm to meet
A friendly place
To drink and eat

And really, almost anytime
There's inspiration for a rhyme
A little ode to café culture
The Kirkgate spirit helps us nurture
An atmosphere of hope and cheer
Community throughout the year

THIS IS THE part of lockdown that I have found the most difficult – not seeing my fellow volunteers and doing my dishwashing and coffee steaming. I'm not good at home with cleaning and organising – this is the hardest thing for me and usually my support workers help me to stay on top of things. Also, my lovely mum usually comes into the café on the day that I work, along with friends and other members of my family. I feel really blessed when this happens.

I love tearooms and coffee shops anyway– either visiting them or working in them. Here is a poem I wrote a number of years ago about a lovely word I discovered, that just summed up how I felt about cafés.

Inglenook

Inglenook is such a lovely word
And of the most descriptive I have heard
Sipping in a village tearoom
In the little corners we can hide
Where the cottage ceilings slope into a combe
And friends and sisters gossip and confide

The stories of the village, street or neighbourhood
Of people who are bad or average or good
Even full blown scandals where the dirt is thrown
And nosy parkers tempted to intrude

So what secrets are exchanged, released, discussed, betrayed?
And consciences, opinions and affections swayed?
Is this a place for politics, love or art?
In the fireside inglenook the story starts

ALSO, THROUGH VOLUNTEERING in the community allotment, in my local area, I have written a lot about nature. Here is one about gardening in Scotland and what the weather is often like – apart from now in this lockdown period. It's been incredibly clement.

Summer in Scotland

Summer's here!
Get out your anoraks and thermal gear
When rain comes gushing
From the grey
With foggy harr throughout the day

The strawberries are waterlogged
And overrun with slugs
Yes, everything becomes a bog
As soon as it is freshly dug

But it's still fun to see the sun
Although the wild wind blows
And through the clouds we still feel proud
How green our grass can grow

So when we see a bumble bee
Roaming in the clover
We can at last take off our hats
The winter's finally over!

IN THIS POEM, when I say *the ugliness of money* – it doesn't mean that I don't want it or need it – but in my own life it has caused so much distress when I have been short of it or had worries about it – and it causes so much argument in the world. I do have a few pairs of shoes and trainers and things, as well as 'stuff' which is unnecessary.

This poem is as much about myself as anybody else, and the extreme fear I have of my own materialism.

Mesmerised

I'm mesmerised by everything I see
Like the ugliness of money
And the beauty of the trees
That manufacture oxygen
For us to breathe
And satisfy all their needs for free

And evolution's creatures in all their glee
Except those who have dominion
Which we think is you and me

We can't help but climb
The mountains, cliffs and trees
And from this we build
The walls and doors and ladders of society

And in every chrysalis the butterfly
Has metamorphosised
It flutters round delightfully
And then it quickly dies

So which of our 'resources'
Are most highly prized?
What will our future wars be over
Gold or bees or flies?
Or water, air or daffodils,
Or muddy paths up in the hills?

As the humble, carefree cockroach
Is despised, yet still survives
It's all a bit bewildering
That's why I'm mesmerised

WILL WE EVER be back to 'normal'. Was normal the problem? I am slowly trying to declutter – but feeling frightened to throw things out in case I ever need them. I suppose I have gone without before, but I need to trust in God or providence – or just the good old human self – not to be surrounded by possessions, - just in case I run out and need them! I will be able to acquire a packet of felt tips again – surely.

Hoarder's Lament

I'm terrified of losing all my socks
Of throwing them and other things away
I know I have a mental block
My stash of stuff just seems to stay and stay

Ten thousand biro pens
A hundred thousand books
Old calendars depicting
A dozen breeds of hens
And stacks of stuff
In crevices and nooks

Six wooden bowls
A china foal
Ten years financial filing
My birthday cards
And yards and yards
Of clothing keep on piling

My littered path
From room to room
Around the bath
A pharoah's tomb

The vast array of shower gel
And scented soap
Make senses swell

My living room
Is full of pants
All hung on radiators
Amid it all, I sit and rant
The clutter generator

The ironing has lain for years
Most things no longer fit me
I have an underlying fear
Reality will hit me

I hate to throw away the old
But I keep buying new
If I were strict, and somewhat cold
Possessions would be few

But I am weak to high degree
A candle in the wind
The clutter monster tempts me
With stuff that should be binned

I'VE ALSO BEEN taking part in an online church service with Liberton Kirk. Loving it and listening to people's interpretations of bible stories. I can never fathom them out when I read them myself. I find it hard to literally believe in the virgin birth and the resurrection, but the idea of universal love and kindness is a welcome thought to most of us and hopefully we can make some of it a reality even some of the time.

God and Me

Two parts of a soul
God and me
Then the holy spirit
Makes us three

Is this the God
That sets us free?

There may be
A thousand trinities
A million eternities

Billions of people
Animals and plants
Is there a place
In heaven for ants?

Apples and tigers
Snakes and spiders
And worldly temptations
Like beers and ciders

Cocaine and wine
Craving is fine
When we're all in the heaven
Of which we've dreamt
The place we mostly
Wish to be sent

Love and beauty
Beyond compare
I look around me
And I'm already there

Dis-ease

Depression is
Today's disease
Sometime's it's backache
Painful knees

Every day
There's something wrong
A feeling that
I don't belong

Worried about my place
In the world
The scheme of things
I'm knotted, curled

It feels infinite
Desperate
Agony
With no respite

Always anxious
What does the world think?
I'm over the ocean
On the brink

Trying to be
At one with life
Yet always on
The edge of a knife

Breaking heart
Feeling got at
Persecuted
Downright flat

I need to set
Myself towards
No regret
A journey forward

Able to say
Life is good
I am okay
Whatever my mood

Looking back

ALTHOUGH THIS PART of the book looks at the past, it also deals with the present and a part of me that I hope is steady and unending.

I come from quite a close family, so when my dad died two years ago we were all devastated, even though we were so very grateful to have had him in our lives. Of course, my mother in particular is the most affected after 62 years of marriage. Here are poems about each of them that I was inspired to write when my dad died.

Beloved Dad

Beloved Dad
Please forgive me for feeling bad
I can't think of much just now
Except for homage towards you

You're free now
Although you never minded
Being bonded
With our amazing earth
The forests, rivers, seas
And all the little burns
Where you tickled trout
All the double shifts you worked
To make sure we didn't go without

The pain you suffered
When people died
The strength you gave us
While you were alive

And now it's you we have to mourn
Something I've dreaded since I was born

But now you're free
And I know you're surrounded
By roses and rowan trees
Aquilegia and sweet peas

Every day, I look for a sign
I know that you're happy
Without pain, just fine

I'll take your example
With all the things that are sent to try us
And try to be kind
Without being pious

I hope I wasn't a disappointment to you
I'm so proud that you were my father

A Flicker

I love your kindness
Your living force
Love how you talk a lot
Watch Poirot and Morse

I know you miss dad
With all your might
Much deeper than sad
Day and night

But you must continue
For some time to come
I'm selfish you see
I need my mum

I love your pride
In my siblings and me
Though sometimes I hide
From your boasting sprees

Immortality
No one can have
There will always be vanity
Good things and bad

Perhaps it's the pain
That makes us strong
Maybe we gain
When things go wrong

Though it doesn't always
Feel like it
We'll recover bit by bit

And when it comes;
Our time to leave
Beautiful earth
People will grieve

And so the cycle
Carries on
back to the earth
Compassionate, strong

Every while
I sense a trigger
A spark of hope
A smile, a flicker
Things may never
Be the same
But remember that
You'll meet again

I HAVE FOUR sisters and one brother – and a brother who died 30 years ago. I wrote a poem about him at the time – which I have somewhere among my untidy files – but can't find. However, here is one that I wrote recently for his 30th anniversary – he would have turned 60 in 2020.

Brother

I always wanted
A little brother
And now I'm older
Old enough
To be your mother

It's thirty years
Since you left
I'm still feeling
Wounded, bereft

I looked up to you
Because you were wild
Remember the fun
Smoking weed
The problem child

How this
Shook my mind
Put me on the road
To being kind

Now I'm looking
At your picture
Young and brave
Much thinner than me
Sweet and naïve

Filmstar looks
Love of music and books
Joyful, peaceful
Articulate, graceful

I'm the older one now
By many years
But losing you still pains me
Brings me tears

Is now my time
To finally grow up?
At fifty five
An eternal pup

If I make it to heaven
Will I find you there?
Free in the wilderness
Without a care

Frozen in time
Forever twenty nine

MANY YEARS AGO, I did yoga daily but got out of the way of it after repeated admittances to hospital and years of disorganisation and illness. For over twenty years I was wary of taking it up again, because I felt it was somehow linked with my illness. In hospital I met people who were quite spiritual and who did yoga. In contrast to this, outside of the hospital I knew no-one who practiced it and they all thought that I was quite a flaky sort of person for taking it up. However, it became more popular and mainstream and it was as if there was an explosion of mind – body practices being developed, talked and written about. Nowadays I use youtube for my yoga classes and I'm back to doing it every day. Although I'm not as physically strong and supple as I was when I was young – I am mentally more relaxed about doing yoga and find that I can practice it even with a western mind and lifestyle. I don't feel inadequate for having a glass of wine or even dare I say – a piece of meat or fish to eat. My goal in the past was to cut these things out completely and I would berate myself for not being strong enough to do so. But I am trying hard to accept myself as a work in progress. Maybe I will manage to achieve my ambitions, but maybe it will take me until I am ninety – either way I am trying hard not to worry about it.

The following are three pieces of prose, which tell the story of an important part of my journey. They are deep in the past and all happened between the ages of 22 and 25. I am not proud of many of my actions, as these pieces give an account of three distinct episodes that I hope I don't have to repeat, even though I know that there are always difficulties in life that I will have to face.

A Sense of Belonging

I remember the dazed, sickly feeling; the heat of the hospital and the gargantuan fear. It had faded slightly on arrival, lurking in the background like a toothache slightly subdued by aspirin. I was angry too, at having made mistakes – big ones and bad ones that would change my life. A lot of the crazy things I had done were because of delusions, but also because of the fear of ending up in a place like this. I had often thought about it during the course of my life, although I was young. Of course the reason I was being admitted was because of these things, but at the time, it was difficult for me to see this clearly.

My parents cried and I remember shouting at them, seeing them as traitors for signing the section paper to commit me. I hadn't washed in weeks and had rarely changed my clothes. My house had been full of rubbish bags, which had dead mice and birds in them that the cat had brought back. There were a lot of maggots at the bottom of the bin and I remember my sisters cleaning the house. My family had started to visit me, finding me in various states of disarray. At one point my parents had been there and called a doctor. She told me I was a pretty girl and had a lot to live for. I was too ill to ask her to take me into hospital – for me that spelled the end life itself. I grabbed one of the kittens that were running around the room and jabbed it with a knife. It squealed in pain and I felt instant shame at the action. I know that later it grew into a very timid cat and was eventually run over by a car. I always felt guilty about it. I have to be honest about this, even though it was a very bad thing that I did.

But at the time, it simply confirmed to me that I was bad – not mad, I cut my arms and legs and even scratched my face with a piece of broken crockery. I kept thinking that I had to die, but thought that I was going to hell because I had been born bad and there was no action I could take other than to burn myself to death – this way I would purge my sins and avoid burning for ever. To say that being brought up a Catholic played a part in this just has to be true. However, having said that, whatever information I had been brought up with, I would have become fanatical about. I was to find out when I went into hospital that a lot of patients became obsessed with religion or outer space and a lot of us thought that nuclear war was imminent. I can remember poring over the Bible, thinking

I could see the afterlife. As well as this, I was always reading horoscopes and using Tarot cards – believing that they predicted the absolute truth. I would watch horror films, believing them to be realistic accounts of life and was generally obsessed with the occult. The line between imagination and reality disappeared and I began to live in fantasy and terror.

I was attracting attention every time I went out, which was unusual for me, and I didn't like it. Looking back, I suppose I must have looked vulnerable. Some of the attention was from well meaning people concerned for my health and welfare, other than that it was from men wanting to have sex. Once or twice I was followed home, and I would fearlessly let people into the house. My flatmate was at the end of her tether with the irresponsible way I was behaving and rightly concerned for her own safety as well. One would-be suitor was a hitch-hiker who left me a gallon of petrol for some reason. I think he said that I could use it as a kind of currency any time I wanted to go hitch-hiking myself, and give it to the driver in return for a lift.

It sat in the corner of my filthy, cluttered bedroom for weeks – I didn't know what to do with it. I didn't do any hitch-hiking but remember being approached by a driver not long afterwards. He asked me if I wanted a lift anywhere and I said yes – I wanted to go through to Edinburgh to see my family as I was living in Stirling and I was finding it hard to get organised enough to go through. I had missed my grandmother's funeral and repeatedly missed the trains to Edinburgh as hours would go by like minutes for me as I sat in a psychotic haze in my little bedroom, smoking and worrying about purgatory and hell. I got into the car and told him that I was going to go and buy cigarettes from the chip shop along the road a bit. When I got the cigarettes I ran out without paying and a few of the shopkeepers chased me out into the street. The car that I was travelling in made a hasty retreat at this point as he obviously didn't want any attention bestowed on him. I later felt as if this was a lucky escape and that I would probably have come to harm if I had stayed in the car.

The days and weeks merged and I lost track of time. I became more and more distant from my flatmate and people around me, and every now and then, someone from my family would appear to see how I was. I later found out that my flatmate had called them because my behaviour by now was so bizarre. I would lock myself out of the flat and put the keys back through the door as I didn't think I deserved to sleep in a bed or have a house or any money or possessions at all. I was also becoming more awkward and less pleasant as my delusions took control.

The final straw was soon to come. I was awake all sorts of odd hours, and I sat up one summer night contemplating suicide and that of course, it had to be done by burning or else I would go to hell forever. I lit a match and set fire to the blankets on my bed with the intention of lying down on top of it until I was dead. But after a brief moment of lucidity I came to my senses and began to realise how stupid and dangerous it was. Then I remembered my flatmate in the next room and smothered the flames. I went out for a walk around 6 am and remember having a cup of coffee in the railway station café. When I returned my flatmate was awake and shouting that I had set the house on fire. She had awoken to find the flat full of smoke with a gallon of petrol in the corner of the room. The blankets must have still been smouldering when I left the house and I didn't realise. This is another thing that I feel better admitting honestly, even though I am deeply ashamed of it.

It was just after this (and mainly because of this) that I was sectioned at the Royal Edinburgh hospital in Morningside. The thing is it took me a while to understand the gravity of what I had done and I still wondered why I was in hospital. I thought that I needed to be punished for what I had done, but alongside this I kept thinking that I was different from other patients and that they had made some sort of mistake. The same as the incident with the kitten – it wasn't on my mind all the time either, and I would forget about it. But during the times when I did remember it, I didn't really know what to do about it and how to make amends. I felt disgusted with myself for the whole episode and contrary to what I originally thought – there wasn't a lot of counselling and psychotherapy in hospital. It was mainly drug treatment.

But while it was a place that had its shortcomings, I did find the hospital to be a sanctuary. I remember walking into the TV room of ward 3 and sitting down next to a pretty blonde woman. She was a little older than me and she poured me a cup of tea and asked me if I wanted a biscuit. I felt an instant sense of belonging, and a feeling that I didn't have to pretend any more.

Silence and Darkness

It's 4 am and the darkness is comforting. There is a constant hum in the background coming from who knows what. I am at home and remembering a time when there only seemed to be silence and darkness. The only noises were the thoughts in my head, berating me for existing. I was having what I believed to be memories of my infancy. Of course, according to the illness, I was an evil child, born bad and destined for damnation – there was no way out. This was the same psychosis that had consumed me before. I had never really stopped believing outlandish things, even though they had given me medication. The thoughts were always lurking in the background, spitefully reminding me that I was alive and that it would take more than pills to help me cope with what was happening to me.

During this time, an acquaintance had been visiting. He would bring with him, second day cakes and sausage rolls from the bakers, and lots of cigarette ends which he must have picked up from the street, or ash trays in pubs. We would eat and drink tea, breaking the cigarette ends into rizlas, reprocessing them into new cigarettes and smoking profusely. I was a heavily addicted smoker by now, after one stint in the mental hospital and being on medication. Unfortunately this seemed to be a particularly common side effect of the entire hospital experience. Even though I had smoked before this, the number of cigarettes I got through in a day – pre mental hospital was less than half of what I now needed. Also the urgency with which I smoked was extremely intense.

I had stopped taking the medication though – mainly forgetting about it after being discharged from hospital and not attending medical appointments. I was back in my flat in Stirling, only about 40 miles from family in Edinburgh, but there was no phone in the flat and it was the 1980s, which meant going to a phone box with a pile of coins to call home. More importantly, nobody could call me and there were no mobile phones. I didn't know much about mental illness, or the importance of medication, but the main thing I remember was my brain being released from its chemical straight-jacket. The bizarre mental meanderings with which I was now faced were both a source of interest and terror to me.

Nowadays I do meditation and yoga in an attempt to find parts of myself which are stronger and somehow more exciting than what I call my 'surface self'. But my current inner world, is a lot steadier and not so engaging and devouring of attention as it was when I was ill. I am thankful of this though, and feel a lot happier now. I still automatically default to expecting the worst in all situations and often phone the Samaritans to help me get through the day.

As life unfolded in those days, it wasn't so much a feeling that it had happened before, but rather that I had foreseen that it would come to pass at an earlier time in my life. This of course was not based on fact, but was part of what would become a web of extremely strange firm beliefs that I would try to run my life in accordance with. I didn't really see any other people except my slightly shifty acquaintance who came round from time to time and had started to make sexual overtures towards me. I started to feel uncomfortable with him and one day, he stole the last ten pounds out of my purse.

I had about a week to survive and really had nobody in Stirling to borrow from. My ex-flatmate, 'H' was in hospital, pregnant with high blood pressure, waiting to give birth and her husband was working every day and visiting her at night. I didn't want to bother them with yet another calamity in my life.

It was at this time that I really became nocturnal. I scoured the streets at night, picking up cigarette ends, as I had several packets of rizla papers in the flat. My clothes were old and tattered and my shoes had huge holes in them. I wore an old sheepskin jacket and looked very much like an old fashioned tramp. There was very little furniture in the flat and no TV, radio or books. 'H' and her new husband had moved my stuff out while I was in hospital, so I had nothing to occupy me except my imagination. I slept very little, even though I was using up a lot of energy walking all night, every night. I wasn't tired.

One time, I remember finding a half eaten packet of crisps, which had been discarded. It was lying on the pavement so I picked it up and ate the contents. I remember eating quite slowly, even though I was very hungry. Another time I found the remains of a bottle of Globe, sun-kool cola. I was a bit afraid to drink it because it could have had anything in it (including pee). But regardless of this it somehow tasted delicious to me and gave a much needed energy boost.

Eventually I didn't even have any tea bags, coffee or even oxo cubes left. My cupboards were completely empty and most days I would just stay in, drink hot water and have a bath. I had opened the padlock which was on the electricity metre with a kirbigrip. There wasn't much money in it as it had been recently emptied, but what there was I spent on tobacco at the beginning of my ordeal, until I was left with one 10p coin. I re-used and re-used this repeatedly and it really gave me as much hot water as I wanted. There was also an electric fire in the flat, so I wasn't completely uncomfortable. Nevertheless, I was aware that I needed food, even though by now, feelings of hunger weren't that much of a problem. I was completely high on exercise from the night walking and lack of body fuel, which must have contributed to my mental state.

It was then that I decided to go down to the little grocer's at the end of the street. The man who owned it was elderly and reminded me of my late grandfather. He had often told me that I could have credit whenever I wanted, and should come into the back shop for a meal with him. He gave me the creeps. However, my situation was getting desperate as giro day approached, and I was getting more and more delusional and spaced out. He gave me five cigarettes and a bar of chocolate. I declined to tell him just how hungry I was and perhaps by this time I was looking the worse for wear, so he didn't invite me into the back shop. I am absolutely sure that this was for the best. The next day I got my 'giro' and bought a jar of coffee and a sweet iced cake. It seemed to fill me up with just a few mouthfuls. I also bought some real, tailor made ciggies for a treat. After all this extreme need, I afforded myself some luxury.

Around this time, my acquaintance came back to see me. I was angry with him for stealing my money and was determined not to let him in. I only opened the door slightly, when he poked his head around it, obviously drunk. I tried to push him away, thinking it would be easy as he was very small. However, to my dismay, he had plenty strength and energy and forced his way in. He twisted my arm up my back and punched me in the face, before shoving me into the main bedroom and locking the door. (both the rooms had keys in them as they were usually rented out as bedsits). He put the key down his trousers and lunged at me, shouting in a rasping, crazed voice, *"I'm going to rape you!"*

Everything felt in slow motion and time seemed to stretch. I began to make a lot of noise, hoping that someone would hear and come to my aid. Of course, this didn't happen so a fist-fight ensued with him getting the better of me. He dragged me to the floor and tried to unbutton my trousers. This was when I had had enough and I turned on him. I am just under 5' 4", but he was probably even smaller and quite thin. I turned the tables and jumped on top of him, putting my knees onto his shoulders and pinned him down. I am not ashamed to admit, that I then wrapped my hands tightly round his throat and bashed his head off the floor. All I could think of was that I was not going to let him rape me. When I let go, he seemed to become sober and sensible. I suppose it was the shock of what I had done to him. He got up, apologised for his behaviour and left the flat. I never saw him again.

This whole experience resulted in a long spell in hospital, once my family got in touch and brought me back to Edinburgh. It has to be said that they got the brunt of my delusions, paranoia and rage, especially my mother, so I have a lot to thank her for. Nonetheless, I was mainly treated with medication and was never really given space to talk about this incident or about the tough physical and psychological conditions I was living in. I wasn't able to open up about it until a few years later and by then the psychiatrist I was seeing wasn't interested, saying that it wouldn't change my diagnosis and nobody was to blame for my illness.

Although this particular hospital experience was pivotal in me making important changes in my life that were to significantly improve it, I have often lain awake at night feeling angry that I was the one who ended up being detained and forcibly injected and stigmatised, while my attacker was free. Mostly though, I just feel sorry for him and the whole incident has melted in my mind. I have forgiven him, mainly because he did apologise and never bothered me again. I sincerely hope that he didn't try this with anybody else. As well as this I now have better relations with psychiatry and see a counsellor once a fortnight.

Coming Home

I had been awarded a furnished tenancy with the council. The flat was painted and carpeted, with a bed, a wardrobe, a cooker, a fridge and a three piece suite. It was so exciting to have the basics of a home all to myself. My family were very pleased and so was I, but still deep inside I was insecure. Yet another episode and admittance to hospital meant that I was definitely going to have to have injections of antipsychotics for the rest of my life.

There was a tug of war within me – one wanting to do it and carry on living – and another that kept planning my suicide, even though there were good things in my life. The injection made me feel ill and bloated. I was sleeping 15 hours a night and apathetic about everything. I felt so insignificant, and tried hard to blend into the background wherever I went but that wasn't to be. People seemed to notice fault with me – often about the way I looked and how low my motivation for everything was.

One person who criticised me a lot was one of my flatmates. He would often tell me I was fat and plain, as well as weak of character and dependant, as if I didn't have a lot going for me. Comments like; *"you look hefty in that dress Anne-Louise"* or *"Could you ever imagine yourself being good looking?"*

I didn't have a lot of confidence anyway, so this type of treatment just reinforced my belief that I was rubbish and worthless. I wasn't even worth giving a token compliment to. The thing that cemented this was one day I was upstairs on a bus (trying to blend into the background), when a young guy started to mock me, *"My God, what a baby you are!"* Before long his friends joined in and they all shouted 'rover' at me over and over again, calling me a dog. As I got up to leave, it felt like the whole bus was shouting at me.

A couple of similar incidents like this led me to the conclusion that it was the medication that made me stand out so much and look so vulnerable. I always gained weight when I took it and It affected the way I walked. My skin was drained of natural colour, and a frugal diet, along with profuse cigarette smoking, seemed to cause blotches and spots on top of this. At a time when I had very low self esteem, the medication felt like a hindrance rather than a solution. I had stopped it twice before, and both times had to be admitted to hospital for long periods until I got back on an even keel (or relative sanity).

Nonetheless, I was taking the medication, confused about the future and depressed about how ugly and stupid and untalented and ungifted I believed I was. Even things I had used to do like arts and crafts, I just couldn't seem to do any more. If I thought it couldn't get any worse, I was sitting up late in the flat one night, about a couple of weeks before I was to move house, when the phone rang. It was my sister, crying, saying that something had happened to our brother 'C'. It turned out he had been sitting on the windowsill of his bedsit at the end of the night, when he slipped and fell. He was killed instantly.

Our whole family was thrown into turmoil and grief. Witnessing my parents' sorrow was almost more than I could bear. Of course we all felt it very deeply, as did cousins and friends, other relatives and colleagues. There was a huge coming together of souls to honour this young life that had been lost. It somehow felt like a sacrifice.

As with all tragedies, some hope always shines through, and for me it was the fact that I forgot about myself and the nasty things people had said and done to me. I was grateful just to be alive. The opinion of a lads' night out wasn't important compared with what had happened. I have always felt guilty that it took something as devastating as this to make me strong. Of course, it's not that I didn't know that this type of bullying was done by shallow people. It was just that I was hurt and upset and embarrassed regardless and even now, I still find it difficult to say that "names will never hurt me".

Soon after the funeral, I moved into my new home. It was near my parents house and in those days they could easily walk it. They visited me shell shocked and grieving. I felt the need to comfort them somehow. Through the natural course of the conversation we got onto discussing the medication. My mum simply asked me to comply with it as they couldn't go through any more heartache. I agreed, and even though I didn't feel very sure, I remembered a woman called 'B' that I had met in hospital and her words of wisdom:

"If you can't do it for yourself, then do it for somebody else!"

I was able to apply this and within a couple years of taking it continually, my body seemed to settle down and I wasn't so zonked. I am now sitting in the same living room, 30 years later, with the candles burning and many little mementos of my time spent here. It has proven to be a haven for me in good times and bad – and I am still on the medication. 26years ago, I had an admittance to the Royal Edinburgh hospital, but have had none since – thanks to the medication – and a lot of great people that have been and are in my life, particularly my partner. We have been together since 1998 and helped to prove that people with problems don't necessarily drag other people down. We don't live together but do love each other. Also, receiving disability benefits has helped me crucially to pay for support to live at home and afford things like bills, internet and food without worry. This is quite controversial in itself though and a source of stress when making applications or going through reviews. Volunteering, along with support workers and medication is my own recipe for my own health as an individual. By themselves they don't suffice for long, and much as I don't want to admit it – the starting point for me was taking the medication regularly. It does have side effects and it is bad for your body – but so does being continually in and out of hospital. I feel as though I am very lucky and really didn't expect to even live this long.

I'm not rich or outwardly successful, but I have a few things going for me – one of them being my life! And yes I am afraid of the Government, DWP, Brexit and the general problems of the world. But I will always remember 'B' – a fellow patient: "If you can't do it for yourself, then do it for somebody else!" When it's applied to things you want to do anyway, like stopping smoking or taking exercise it can really give you motivation to think of somebody else who wants the same thing for you.

These three little essays may seem as though they aren't really relevant to the overall collection. Although some experiences don't really inspire me to write poetry they still motivate me to write. I feel as though they are important and have to be mentioned. They have shaped my attitude towards life, and made me grateful for the good things I've got. I have depression, anxiety and schizophrenia but this doesn't mean that I'm unhappy. I take pleasure in nature including human nature, although I'll admit I'm often dismayed by the the things that we humans do when we're being bad. War, children being murdered, racism, terrorism, and just general lack of compassion amongst people. This is where my support workers and the Samaritans can really help, and I have accepted that this is the kind of support that I think I will always need.

I use facebook for posting my poetry and keeping in touch with old friends. Sometimes I share posts of nature and other times petitions that I have signed. I sometimes rile people with this, although it is not meant. I have had some nasty retorts to my more political posts on facebook and I wonder if it is worth it to continue, but most of the time my poetry has largely good responses – so that keeps me going. This is the most important thing. I believe that everything has a purpose and can be used for good or ill. I try to use facebook for the good and have decided that perhaps politics is not the most sensible use of it. I tend to favour policies that support the NHS and the welfare state – because of my experience of life. Many years ago I worked part time and qualified for tax credits. However, the rules have changed so much and the reviews of benefits is so frequent that I am too anxious to take on paid work and so I stick to my volunteering.

I EVENTUALLY MANAGED to stop smoking in January 2013 but this is the way I used to think of myself – that I was not going to heaven with all the good folk! They didn't smoke and drink and call helplines because they were suicidal. They weren't slackers who wiled away their days in idyllic community gardens and coffee shops. They were workers and often they let me know that.

All Souls

Is there a party in the sky?
Where all the good souls flit and fly
Around about the stars and sun
Dancing on rainbows and having fun

And all the mere mortals like us
Who suffer from greed and sloth and lust
Where do we go after death?
Once we've breathed our final breath

Is there a party somewhere else?
Or will we be all by ourselves?
Mopping floors and stacking shelves
Working our way up the ladder
From limbo where the folk are sadder

But I would say that I am glad
To be ordinary and sometimes mad
Than living in a perfect dream
Trying to be society's cream

Having it all

Grant me chastity and continence
But not yet
Freedom to roam without penance
And in no one's debt

Clean fingernails and habits
Without contradiction
Indulging in life's titbits
With no sordid addictions

Let me feel the glow of lust
And purr with compliments imparted
But help me do the things I must
To carry on the work I've started

All that glitters is my passion
Food and wine and gold
Let me have this in a fashion
But save my soul before I'm old

In fact I want to have it all
No Cinderella's rags for me
But I need magic grit and gall
If I am ever to be free

Tar

Diamonds on the water
Toddlers on the sand
Golden retrievers running
Cigarette in my hand

Another stop for nicotine
Numb bum, stiff knees
Touring in our limousine
Around the villages by the sea

And every other hour or so
I must have this little break
To replenish stocks of nerve gas
And munch on tea and cake

Driving round the castles
And seeing yachts in sail
How I'll enjoy the photos
Of my trip to the coast of Wales

In almost every one of them
I'll be outside the car
Gasping over my addict's crutch
O how I need my tar!

Glasses

Spent exactly 20 minutes
Looking for my glasses
I had just taken them off
And they were spirited away

I started swearing, rummaging
Floating from room to cluttered room
Stalking my glasses

Finding other things
That I had lost aeons ago

Thinking of my grandmother
Her front parlour
Polished vases and gleaming brass
Numerous nick nacks
Each one in its own dust-free space

No piles of paper
Flipping and flopping
Over the edges of tables and chairs
Or pouring out from wardrobes and cupboards

The comforting glow
Of polished metal, glass and porcelain
Still brings pleasure to me

Shining wood and silver
Filter little bursts of joy
Into my muddled mind
They help me reminisce
About times
When I felt secure

Watching Princess Anne's wedding
To Mark Phillips
On a black and white television
In Drumdryan Street
The smell of brasso and beeswax around me
Carrots and leeks bubbling away in the soup

Looking for my glasses
Led me to remember
An innocent time of life
Far more ordered than now

Looking forward

THIS IS THE future part of the story. Sometimes I would like to strive towards gaining qualifications, or employment or even marriage to my partner. But really what I want to strive towards is love and happiness. It's true that I need food and clothing and shelter – as well as books and wine and a trip to the theatre or an internet connection so that I can keep in touch with people using my computer. Money and material things are just so important to me and I know that I wouldn't be able to do my volunteering if I couldn't easily keep myself clean and warm and clothed and fed. I have to say that looking after the planet and increasing the little pockets of nature that I see in my environment are what I want to work towards in life.

Recipe for a melting moment

Take several drops of rain
And a pint of sunshine
Toss them onto a wet balcony
And sauté
Making sure that you remember
To add a spoonful
Of spider's web

Stir well until it turns a golden colour
And leave to settle

Then take a large bowl
Of mother earth
Add a handful of laughter seeds
While a plump pigeon is cooing
In the background among the weeds

Next, blend all the ingredients together
Into a compassionate heart
Finely chop a good bunch of unconditional love
And whisk to create a melting moment

Sublime!

I LOVE THE weeds growing through the cracks in the paving, and seeing nature blossoming in the city. I think that there are a lot of people keeping bees in the city nowadays because our parks and gardens offer so much flora. Seeing animals is a real treat, and sometimes my neighbours see the fox that lives somewhere around our back green. I have only had this pleasure once but there were two of them at the same time. This was just after my father had died and I took it as a real sign that he was with me.

At the start of a new day

I woke up early, as I had every day since dad's death. I found it difficult to lie at peace in the morning when the mind monkeys started. Sometimes they were there at night as well when I went to bed, panicking my sleep. I had started to wake up feeling as if I needed a brandy for breakfast, my whole system aching with grief.

The pains in my bones had subsided though, and I could sit cross-legged on the floor again, albeit with a little padding under each knee. I can't remember when the sun rose, but suddenly I noticed it was light and I heard barking outside as I sipped my morning coffee – a rush of dopamine. Although the mornings were particularly marred by emotional pain, there was something about the first light that brought joy, even though I was anxious and grieving.

I decided to go and investigate the barking. The couple on the ground floor have a pug, which has a persistent, squeaky bark. This was far weightier, like a bigger dog of some kind. I crept up to the window, not sure what to expect. There is another neighbour who sometimes looks after a rotweiler. It is friendly and well cared for, but still triggers a pang of fear in me.

The shared back green had little separated patches of lawn, and right in the middle of it stood a beautiful vixen. She was so poised and elegant, with her auburn fur and bright piercing eyes. She looked as if she was smiling. The fence had come down and there were little breaks in the hedges between the gardens. She trotted nimbly between them and her mate, a handsome dog fox waited good naturedly in the garden opposite. It was as if the vixen was marking territory as she walked between the fences, peeing occasionally. I would have expected this of the dog, but I think she was in season.

This went on for a good few minutes. She walked around and nuzzled up to the dog fox, who remained still. I watched unseen from behind my living room window for about 10 minutes, until finally they eloped together across the backgreens.

Sometimes I look outside early in the morning, hoping they will come back, but perhaps I am being greedy. Although foxes are common in the town, this was a delightful and special experience. Maybe if it happened all the time, it wouldn't be so magical any more. Although somehow I think it would.

I said to my partner that the first thing I thought of was to tell my dad about them.

My partner said, *"He put them there!"*

A poem about ageing

I'm in love with ageing
Beautiful bags, ravishing wrinkles
Double chins, puffy eyes

Youth can't last forever
But love goes on and on

Bunions, arthritis, inertia
Daily denture baths
And dare I say – dementia?

How can we embrace all this
And beat the mid-life blues
Do we have control of it
Through the path choose?

Would we really want to be
A beautiful youth?
Full of life and innocent truth

When I was young
I struggled with my sanity
Couldn't really see life's opportunity
Completely lost my grip on reality

But now that I am middle-aged
I've reached a much more happy stage
I can see things as they are
And just be glad I've come this far

BETWEEN AGEING AND extinction, I'm not sure what kind of future we humans have on the earth. I'm not of the opinion that climate change is a fallacy and that continually cutting down rain forest and drilling for oil is not of any harm to the planet. I feel responsible myself as I use heating in my house and ride in buses. I don't drive, but I get driven to places by car, and I also have quite a nice life, although I am ill. I want things to be better for the youth and their children. I want human life to go on.

Us

We've only been here
For a blink
Hardly time
To stop and think
But soon we could
Become extinct

Wise walker
Earth stalker

Plastic, petrol
Concrete, tar
Going everywhere
By car

Pesticides and pollution
Attacking is
Our every solution

After 13 billion years
We finally arrive
And full of hopes and fears
Begin to strive

Inventing technology
Defying biology

Hardly ever harmonious
Battles home and abroad
Believing that they're glorious
And in the name of God

Perhaps one day
We will implode,
Become one
Maybe then we will be done

Will anyone leave a legacy?
A story to be told?
When there is no food left
Just hunger and cold

Back to Eden
Finally, the truth
Instead of seeking immortality
And of course, unending youth

I HAVE ALWAYS worried about homelessness, what with having mental health problems. It's not so much guilt I feel when I see people begging but really 'there but for the grace of God' I always feel a pang thinking; 'how would I ever be able to deal with that situation?'

Festive Pie

The stars on the glitter tree are bright
Star of wonder, bursting with light
Looming in the corner
Delighting the room
Alleviating a little of
The winter gloom

Sparkling reindeer
Tinsel, snowing
Scented candles
Warm and glowing
Plastic santas
Round and fat
Jacket furry
Pom-pom hat

And yet I worry
About my flat
Paying bills
Amid the joyous
Christmas thrills

Buying gifts
Wine and food
Will God ever
Think I'm good

As I stroll past people
Bedding down
Deep in doorways
Around the town

How close are we all
To a bed on the street?

Shivering
Wet clothes and feet

There but for providence,
Go I
As I tuck into my festive pie

Writing

A lot of people write
When they're depressed
Sometimes they paint
Or sculpt or draw
Or sing their feelings
Rough and raw

It's a way they have
Of dealing with distress

Some people drink
To quell the pain
Or shop, have sex
Wear Prada sunspecs
And squander
All their money on cocaine

Other people like to walk
Or run in circles
Round the block
Keep fit, Pilates
Drink skinny lattes

Or there are those
Who simply like
To sit and talk

Each time I crunch Doritos
Or sip on alcoholic drink
Prosecco and mojitos
It causes me to sit and think

That though I numb my pain
And suffer dark depression
I'm still alive and sane
And every hour's a lesson

Love and Money

Got to mention
Love and money

Are they really real?
Can we survive
And stay alive
Without our daily meal?

With only feelings
To sustain us
Stories, music, art
Ideas, prayer
Meditation
Our inner soul
Our dedication
Is this the place to start?

Is love as serious
As money?
Is it needed
More than food?

I know that without
Love at heart
Nothing can be good

But do we need
Our pretty things
Houses, cars and diamond rings?

As lovers twinkle
Tease and touch
Is money needed
Just as much?

When I am hungry
And alone
I yearn for love
And food and home

A little perfume
Now and then
Luxury for
Women, men
Warmth and wine
A place to dine

But after death
Eternal sleep
There is nothing
We can keep

Except our love
For one another
That's why
It's worth our while
To smother
(each other in love)

National Identity

I'm Scottish, British, European
English speaking
Earthling

With rough hands
Holding my coffee cup
Feel like I'm dancing on quicksand

I sometimes watch television
And I'm on a mission
To improve health and happiness
Wherever I go
Filling people with goodness
From the plants that we grow

I want to reclaim my Scottishness
From SNP
My Britishness from Brexit
And I'm still European
In fact I'm all three
I walk in the world as a human
Carefree

I like living in my body
With its mousy hair
Stiff joints and pallid skin

I don't want to be better looking
Taller, or excessively thin

But sometimes I despair
At the story of my race
And wonder what reprisals
We can expect to face

From the relentless pursuit of domination
Not content to give a contribution
But killer, exploiter, manipulator, thief

Everywhere we went
We had to be chief

What is wrong with being equal?
I worry that
Destruction
Will be our sequel

I'm not saying that we are all bad
But we can't let go
Of the power we had

And being the big fish in the pond
Not noticing
The miles of ocean
Out there and beyond

Bury my heart at Wounded Knee
A story that is painful to me

I knew my people had done wrong in the past
I just didn't know how far we had gone
Or how long the damage would last

For Addicts

Don't despair at loneliness
Desolation and gloom
Or think you're any less a person
For staying in your room

As long as there's a window
And even if there's not
You're still here in the world

As Odysseus was
And all the great adventurers
Leaders and archetypes of strength
Who resisted temptation
And have been around for centuries
In schoolrooms and universities
Stimulating grey matter and debate
Inspiring new philosophies
From the ancient timeless

But you've as much right to be here
As them or anybody else
In the lively, living places
Like cafés, libraries, colleges,
Galleries, supermarkets
Sports arenas
Planes, trains and automobiles
And at sea with your intrepid crew

And maybe one day
Your story will inspire people
In schoolrooms and universities

The one who was curious

Lured by sirens
Seduced by nymphs
And swept away by hideous monsters
During the tempest

And however bare
Your empty cell may seem to be
Remember that all those people
In the lively, living places

Return to the same emptiness
Where there's just themselves
And no jobs, no money
No chocolate, no religion
No music, no drugs, no alcohol
No books, no family, no friends
No fast black ship, no crew

Some are joyful here
Some ill at ease
But there's no shame in either

And if your tormentor weakens you
And you start to feel you'll never cope
And you churn with fear
It's then you need to tell yourself
That this is your life force
And your single ember of hope

Mrs Blue

Blue is your favourite colour
It's boyish, it's cool
And it pertains to a certain football team

To you, it's a vibrant and carefree colour
Rousing and regal
It brings out your warmth

Yet for me it's the colour of loneliness
Of icicles on the inside of the bathroom window
Of Conservative politics
Of my pendulum moods
And everything cold and unfriendly

But lately I've noticed
That it brings out the best
In my mid brown hair and hazel eyes
And makes my slightly ruddy complexion look clear

It's the colour of
Lobelia dangling over hanging baskets
And hot summer skies
Kingfishers and Persian cats
And newborn babies' eyes

The ink in my pen
And smart naval uniforms
Of irises, crocuses
And sometimes the ocean itself
Which is where we were all born

It's everywhere I look in the world
Lowering the temperature
Of my worried, sleepless nights
My disappointment, frustration and petulance
It's the indigo outside night time
Of mystery, silence and forgiveness

Neighbours

I hear my neighbours
Pottering around
Doing homely things
Making wholesome sounds
It's comforting, I've found

Mowing the grass
In our back green
Mopping
Keeping the stair clean

Putting the recycling bins out
Plugging in the hoover
The washing machine spins around
And the tumble drier, crease smoother

Conversation echoes in the stairwell
Checking on each other's health
None of us are rich and famous
Our friendship is our wealth

And living in our tenement
There's nobody that I resent
For being well-to-do
I find that I am quite content
And I have the most fantastic view

Skin deep

Rapunzel, let down your mousy hair,
With its salt and pepper streaks,
Split ends and widow's peak.
Let down your guard
And let go
Don't be strange
Let it flow

Skin Deep

I'm a plain person – medium build, mousy hair and perhaps if I was more outstanding in one way or another I would have different opinions about beauty and the beauty industry, but I'm easy come, easy go. When I was in my youth I wore lots of mini skirts, bikinis and short shorts. I had fun with clothes and make up, but now that I'm in my fifties, it's a relief to not be worried about what my legs look like – and not be wearing the same styles as I did then. For some reason I am not in the running for compliments or criticism nowadays and I think it is because I am post menopausal.

Maybe it is to do with the people who are in my life now, but they don't constantly comment on my weight the way they used to, or mention my appearance as much as they did, and as a result my perception of beauty has changed. I have false teeth, wrinkles and a double chin – and I'm proud of them. There is no way that I'm as pretty as I was but then I don't think I was particularly pretty anyway. I remember in those days, not wanting to be affected by criticism or flattery but I was. My attractiveness depended very much on the state of my health and I wasn't really in control of this. Nor am I now. I can affect my life but I'm not in complete control of it.

When I was in my early twenties, I was often in the Royal Edinburgh Hospital. There was a woman that I didn't know very well, but used to see sometimes on the ward and her face was badly burned by some sort of accident. This used to frighten me, as not only did it make you look different, it was also a very painful thing – a burn and I used to wonder how I would cope if it were to happen to me. But then for some reason I expected difficulties in my life and for bad things to happen, I still do to some extent because this is life – but I definitely don't worry as much about how I look as I did when I was younger.

Now in Covid 19 pandemic, many people, men and women are wearing face coverings and it has become mandatory in enclosed public places. It seems now that being handsome or beautiful is not as important as it was and that it is more important to be healthy. Muslim women have often been criticised for wearing veils and I will admit that this is not a practice I intend to take up myself – it is very different from the way I have lived and expressed myself. However, I do not intend sign up for botox injections or breast enhancement surgery either, as it is just not for me. It doesn't mean that these things are wrong or that I disapprove of them particularly. Both seem at opposite ends of a seesaw to me – with myself somewhere in the middle - but perhaps they're not. Maybe if there is coercion or pressure involved, but if either of these practices is someone's normality – who am I to say that it shouldn't be?

I am lucky to have a nice partner, who seems to think I'm beautiful, even though I take my teeth out before I go to bed and I have a lockdown belly at the moment. This is possibly because we have been together a long time and grown fond of each other's supposed inadequacies, and one thing I am glad about now, is that I see the beauty in imperfection. Although, I do own up to reading a bit of celebrity gossip on my phone , I'm not much interested in Khloe Kardashian or lady Gaga and their latest look. I really just read for light-hearted respite from the world's seriousness and these people may well be glamorous but the people I see at the bus stop and in the supermarket are just as easy on the eye as far as I am concerned.

I know that it might be a cliché, but I think it is nice to see character in a face and a little wear and tear in a body – including my own. Now that I am growing older I am not so afraid of it. Beauty really is in the eye of the beholder, passes with time and is only skin deep. It is good to appreciate beauty for what it is, but it can also cause as much unhappiness as it does enjoyment when we afford it more importance than it deserves. It really is to do with health and nature and diversity. The following piece is about health and beauty and how they are linked.

PARTIALLY ON THE subject of beauty, I don't usually give people a row for smoking and extoll the virtues of being an 'ex-smoker,' but after looking through some photographs of myself, I came to the conclusion that stopping smoking is a major life's achievement and one of the best things I ever did. I wouldn't deliberately pressurise people who may be finding life tough and feel that quitting smoking is not even on their radar. Rather, I would like to help people who are 'ready' for quitting, knowing that even if it took a few attempts, it would eventually fall into place for them.

As I have said, I am not an excessively vain person, but I do put my false teeth in before going out and I do yoga each day as much for my body as my mind. I don't have to think of myself as being beautiful in order to feel good about myself – I am happy to just be okay. Nonetheless, even I am pleased with my appearance a few years after giving up smoking. Here is the 'before' photo of me around 2012 approximately aged 47, just about 6 months before giving up.

As you can see, I have not inserted my denture here, and I am smoking a cigarette, first thing in the morning.

Still smoking; 2012

Although this is a particularly bad photo, the difference in my appearance a few years later aged 51 is quite astounding and there is no airbrushing, make-up or botox involved. Just a bit better food, a new, complete set of top dentures and three and a half years clear of smoking.

I wasn't able to save myself from the gum disease that caused my teeth to fall out, even after I stopped – it was too far gone but I haven't had any abscesses since then and the constant low-grade pain has subsided.

I was the 14 year old girl who used to put lipstick on and 'practise my smoking' in front of the mirror, convinced it would make me glamorous and thin. In fact it was to make me a bedraggled old hag who was abused in the street and the Edinburgh Botanics by middle class women and men – yummy mummies in particular – and their friends, as I tried to blend into the background of things and go unnoticed with my anti-social habit. This was meant as a kind of deterrant I think, but at the time, it just upset me so much that I reached for yet another cigarette. I am not keen on this kind of social rejection, particularly when I am the brunt of it! I believe people need encouragement more than tough love, or at least, something to go towards as well as something to run away from.

I also spent many years as a smoker, looking okay but in my forties, it became like a race to try to stop the gum disease. But, rather than be upset about losing my teeth, I feel that it makes life more interesting. I would say to people – don't be afraid to be imperfect – and don't be afraid of putting on weight. I put on over a stone when I stopped but that is what my body needed. Some people actually lose weight and others stay the same. Your body will just get healthier.

At Redhall Walled Garden with new lambs; Spring, 2016

Journey of wellbeing

I DON'T HAVE any qualifications to speak of, nor do I have my 'own philosophy' on life. I have tried to survive and sometimes do a little better than that and actually gain fulfilment from the activities and that I take part in. My occupations as a gardener and catering assistant are fulfilling, although I find it hard to organise myself and really be confident with people.

The next few poems are just for fun. They come from writing exercises that we tried at my writing group. I won't bother explaining all the details – hopefully they will make you smile a little. Laughing and smiling are important for wellbeing and in my opinion, worth striving towards.

Oliver Twist in Nigella's kitchen

Oliver Twist
His breakfast he missed
The gruel was all gone
When he came along
There was nothing to make him
Big and strong

So this wimpy kid
In the garden he hid
Stole a turnip for food
And away he slipped

A small boy in rags
With no luggage or bags
Made his way to the city
Seeking fortune, not pity

And as he sat among the pigeons
Nigella spied him, from her kitchen

Was he on junk?
Had he done a bunk?
Her curiosity was aroused
So she grabbed some food
And out she pounced

"Do have some spelt rigatoni
With wild garlic and walnut pesto!
Perhaps some pulped avocado?
And of course, rack of lamb
Marinaded in oregano, cranberry seeds and truffle oil.
Then some raspberry and rhubarb compote
With spiced ewes yoghurt
All washed down with some turmeric tea?"

Ollie thought that he was dead
And this was happening in his head
"Where is love?" he was so sad
Nigella felt guilt for the things she had
"But my cooking really isn't bad"

"I see the life for which you've opted,
And you look as though you need adopted."
So Ollie said "I wouldn't mind,
You look so beautiful and kind"

Nigella bought some fish and meat
And said "You certainly need to eat.
I think we'll both get on a treat!

"We can start by cooking lots of food
And you can promise to be good"

"I will" he said "You're just so cool,
But please don't send me to boarding school
I've suffered enough from institutions
That's what brought me to destitution."

"I'll wash the pots and sweep the floor
And always, always ask for more."

Glamour Puss

My sister's buddy came to stay
A pampered princess
Not a stray
I thought I'd sit with her and play
But very soon
Was chased away

The rudest guest I've ever met
I thought I'd spoil her
She'd be my pet

But every time I passed her by
She'd let out a ferocious cry
Hissing, spitting, claws extending
No chance of stroking and befriending

A warrior feline, sleek and slight
Slinking around during the night
Pouncing out from underneath
Snarling and baring teeth

So I'll just tell my sister – "well"
"Your companion is the guest from hell
I thought we'd get along just swell
But her temper I just couldn't quell"

She's such a pretty girl too
Saucer eyes of green and blue
Silken hair, black and white
Springing easily and light
From floor to couch to windowsill
Looking out for something to kill

This cutest ever glamour puss
Is really a demon on the loose

Slim Jim's Terriers

Inka and Skye
Mother and son
Two cutie pies
And full of fun

Together they make
The perfect team
They go for walks
And sleep and dream

Inka, so mature and wry
She's sensible compared to Skye

But still she likes
To chase the crows
And squirrels, which
Could bite her nose

But over and above all
Inka, just adores her ball
"Grr, it's mine – you cheeky swine"

Yet Skye can
Get along just fine
Playing with lots
Of different toys
And other dogs
– A friendly boy!

Of course,
He's really not the brightest
His brain is definitely lightest

These two terrific doggies
Scamper, sprint
And chase the moggies

They are just
The best of friends
And one another
They'll defend

With slim Jim
Their loyal master
Each day they grow
Fitter and faster

Chasing cats and birds and balls
While Jim co-ordinates it all
Hiking over hills and glens
Looking after his little friends

Halloween

I'm no a charity ya spilte wee brats
Yis pick oot ma hoose among a' these flats
Jist tae torment mi wi trick or treat
Aye wantin money or somethin tae eat

But what de yis dae bit wear plastic fangs
And nylon outfits fae Matalan
Yis might tell me that I'm an auld witch
But at least a ken how tae make and stitch

Yis cannae sing or dance at a'
Standin like stooges against the wa'
Yis dinnae even ken how tae dook
And a never see yis eatin fruit
So what guid are aepples and nuts tae yoos
Another few years
Ye'll be oan the booze

And now looking forward to the new year; a little poem on the 1ˢᵗ of January

01.01.2021

Lockdown hogmanay
A special day
Old year's gone
Passed away
The Covid virus
Please don't stay
Get vaccinated
Hope and pray

I wonder what
Will wipe us out?
And what will kill our trees?
Ash dieback, sudden oak death
And Dutch elm disease
Our ecosystem balances
With tigers, plants and bees

I wonder what the future brings
Can we work it out?
Let's hope that 2021
Will help to ease our doubt

Allay our fears
This Brexit year
Who can tell the future
Remembering that all the time
We are part of nature

I'm guilty as anything
Guilty as can be
I worry about money
As nothing comes for free